Amongst The Gods
A Polytheist Prayer Book

Introduction:

As a hellenic polytheist, I became obsessed with what I refer to as the "lesser gods". Those who walk the Earth amongst us and those who have fallen into shadow behind the powerful figures of those that reside on Olympus. I wanted to write prayers to these gods, because in my personal beliefs, gods and mortals work on a circular system of dependence. We depend on them to aid us through life and they in turn depend on us for prayers, worship, sacrifice to sustain their divine bodies. This book went through stages as I began to write it. At first it was meant to be a personal devotional to the "lesser gods" so that I could form a pattern of offering up worship to them. While writing that, I decided it made more sense to write a prayer book to as many Hellenic deities as I could find. Not long after that decision, it became clear to me that this personal prayer book needed to be in the hands of anyone who would like to have it. This is my absolute labor of love for my religious beliefs and the gods who sit at the top of it all. I hope that this book helps you form stronger relationships with the gods and peaks your interest in the "lesser gods".

Sadly some of those mentioned do not have many stories left for us to hear. Some have none at all. Nevertheless, I have tried diligently to do them justice and offer them worship. Some of these prayers may have content that you do not immediately understand without context. This has been done purposefully to encourage you to explore and learn on your own about these deities and their lives. As you say these prayers, take comfort in knowing that they are hearing you and that you are helping to sustain a custom that stretches far back into time into what would now feel like a completely different world. A world where mortals saw the gods in everything. I crave to return back to a time like that where everything carries higher meaning, I want us all to find what's most important for us. To feel real nature, to experience real divine intervention and for every single one of us to walk amongst the gods.

How To Use This Book:

I have laid this book out to give you 147 days in a row of prayer. If this is the way you choose to use it, then you are using it as intended. However, I am not one to tell people who to pray to, how to practice their beliefs, or how to worship. You should use this book however feels right to you. If that means skipping to a deity you are working with or feel close to, then do that. If it means reading one prayer a week, or four in one day, then do that. This is not an assignment or a requirement, it is simply written to aid those who are looking for it. I have written these prayers fairly short so that everyone will feel comfortable setting aside time to pray and not feel that the task is daunting. Set aside a whole day dedicated to each god, or just a few minutes in the morning or evening to say your prayer. The choice is yours.

Day One
Achelois
Moon Goddess/ Source of comfort and healing

Achelois of the moon, hear our plea. Bring us comfort and good health through hard times. Guide us with your wondrous light. Move the leaves and ring the chimes so we may open our ears to your divine inspiration.

Day Two
Achelous
Patron God of the Achelous river and freshwater

Achelous, mighty god of the river. We recognize you in all your forms. The bull headed, the centaur, the merman with coiling tail, and the man. We ask you to drink from your pitcher so that we may be sustained. Allow us to walk amongst the creatures that come to your banks so we may speak your name and drink.

Day Three

Aeolus

Keeper of the wind/ King of Aiola

Mighty Aeolus, king of Aiola, keeper of the winds. Place us in your favor. Provide us with favorable wind and keep the storms at bay. May they stay locked away on Aiola and not find our shores.

Day Four

Aether

God of light and the atmosphere

Aether of primordial light. Breath of the gods, keeper of the skies. May your air stay clean, may your light shine bright, and may your skies blaze blue.

Day Five
Alastor
The avenger of familial feuds and bloodshed

Alastor, guard us from those closest to us who would stand against us. Help us avenge ourselves against those who would turn on their own blood, who would dishonor their own home. Cleanse us of them and those who stand with them.

Day Six

Alcyone

Associated with peace/ turned into a halcyon bird by Zeus

Alcyone, the self drowning, who threw herself into the ocean for her lost love, we pray that you find peace. May your days as a halcyon be spent by calm waters. Please bestow the peace you find upon the ones we love and warn us of the wrath of the gods.

Day Seven
Alectrona
Goddess of the sunrise/ awakening from slumber

Alectrona, goddess of sunrise. We thank and praise you for allowing us to wake. May we not waste this day we have been given, but instead be inspired by your warming rays of morning to live each day to the fullest potential. For one day the fates will no longer allow you to wake us from slumber.

Day Eight
The Algea
Goddesses of pain/ anguish/sorrow/grief

Immortal Algea. Lupe, Ania, and Achus. You visit often throughout our mortal lives. We see you at birth and at death. May you visit us only when necessary and guide us through our grief when we must experience it.

Day Nine
Amphitrite
Goddess and Queen of the sea

Amphitrite, queen of the sea, oldest of the naiads. We thank you for the bounty of your waters. We vow to protect your creatures in your honor. Please guide us to safe harbors with your protection and blessings.

Day Ten
Antheia
Goddess of flowers, vegetation, gardens

Antheia, goddess of blooms, we thank you for your flowers. The bees drink from them and spread your gifts through our world. Please bless our gardens and the food you help put on our tables so that we may eat in your honor.

Day Eleven
Aphaea
Associated with agricultural fertility

Aphaea, favored by Artemis. We thank you for your blessings of fertility. May our farms always prosper under your watchful eye.

Day Twelve
Aphrodite
Goddess of love/ beauty/ sex

Aphrodite, the beautiful, born of the sea. Grace us with your blessings. Help us to find love, but to also love ourselves. To be beautiful on the inside as well as the outside. Help us to find lovers that make us experience true ecstasy. Your beauty alone blesses all of us and we thank you endlessly for the gifts you bestow upon us.

Day Thirteen
Apollo
God of archery/ music/ prophecy/ healing and disease/ the sun/ poetry

Mighty Apollo, god of the sun, slayer of python. With your chariot, you bring life to our world as you pull the sun each day. Help us to see through the darkness of our own lives through your divine prophecy. Help us to heal from our ailments and keep disease outside of our doors. For you are truly bright and majestic, bringing with you joy and happiness.

Day Fourteen
Arachne
Mother of spiders

Arachne, mother of spiders, we will remember your story whenever we see a spider's web. We will remember your skills on the loom, but also to not fall prey to hubris and incur the wrath of the gods.

Day Fifteen
Ares
God of courage and war

Ares, son of Zeus and the queen, Hera. Give us the courage to stand against those that would threaten us. Release your ever burning anger and bloodlust on our enemies, leading us always to victory.

Day Sixteen

Aristaeus

God of beekeeping/ shepherds/ taught many arts by the gods

Aristaeus, who learned much from the gods. He who saved the bees through sacrifice. We honor and thank you greatly for teaching mortals the knowledge to thrive and prosper. May you be honored every time we use your knowledge to ensure our survival.

Day Seventeen
Artemis
Goddess of the moon/ hunting/ protector of children

Artemis, the chaste, goddess of the moon . We look to you for guidance in the darkest night. We bathe in your light and bask in your energy. Please guide us to the things we need. Please protect our children from harm with your graceful hand. Your kindness, we shall always remember.

Day Eighteen
Asclepius
God of medicine/ necromancer/ placed in the stars after death

Asclepius, the serpent holder. He who was placed amongst the stars. We look to you in our days of sickness and unrest. Grant us good health and help keep us from the banks of the styx for as long as the fates and the gods allow it.

Day Nineteen
Astra Planeta
Gods of the five wandering stars

Phainon. Phaethon, Pyroeis, Eosphoros, and Stilbon. Those who dive into the world river in front of the sun. You watch over Earth and all of it's inhabitants. May you wander free forever.

Day Twenty

Astraea

Goddess of innocence/ associated with justice

Astraea, star maiden. We beg for your return. Once you walked among us and we wait for you to do so again. Bring an end to our suffering. Take away the blackness and make us innocent once again.

Day Twenty One
Ate'
Goddess of mischief/ delusion/ ruin

Ate', the great mischief maker. If you must bring ruin down upon the heads of man, be it not brought upon the defenseless, but rather those who defy and insult the gods. Crush power instead of poverty and be honored in this way.

Day Twenty Two
Athena
Goddess of strategy/ wisdom/ crafts

Mighty Athena, who sprouted fully armored from Zeus' head. She who gave the olive tree to Athens. Goddess of wisdom and strategy, guide us through our own personal battles, so that we may make sound decisions and not be overcome by blood lust. Instill in us great wisdom so that we may use it to honor the gods.

Day Twenty Three
Atlas
Holder of the sky/ personifies endurance

Atlas, he who was condemned to hold the sky aloft, we recognize you as a symbol of great endurance and strength. We should only hope to carry the same endurance through our own trials and tribulations. May you come to peace with the king of Olympus and find rest.

Day Twenty Four
Atropos
The fate that chooses the death of mortals/ cutter of life thread

Atropos, the inflexible one. Holder of the shears. We pray to you. We ask that our life thread not be cut prematurely and if you will it, that our passing be painless and quick. The fates are truly great and all, no matter if god or man must answer to you and your sisters.

Day Twenty Five
Attis
God of vegetation/ associated with rebirth

Attis, who castrated himself in frenzy, who spilled his blood upon the land. You stand now as a mighty fir. You bless us with beautiful land. Through transformation, you were reborn as we all wish to be. To become something more than ourselves and feed the land.

Day Twenty Six
Bia
Goddess of force/ power

Bia, who sits in silence. We honor and respect you for taking on the task of enforcing the gods will. For fighting in the war with the titans and for being one of Zeus' most trusted. Guide us in learning to use our own force strongly and appropriately.

Day Twenty Seven
Boreas
God of the north wind/ bringer of winter

Boreas, as your mighty wings flap, they bring with them the wind that chills the bones. Spare us from your temper. Your great strength is known, and your powers respected. Allow us to revel in your chill as it covers and overtakes all.

Day Twenty Eight

Brizo

Goddess of dreams/ protector of mariners

Brizo, we pray to you for your protection. Be it in the sea or in slumber. Help us to navigate what we face. Help us to understand that which we dream and see clearly the messages laid before us.

Day Twenty Nine

Caerus

God of luck and opportunity

Caerus, who brings opportunity to those who are deserving. Grant us good fortune in our endeavors. Allow us to recognize the signs when you are allowing us a chance to seize what we seek.

Day Thirty
Calliope
Muse of epic poetry

Calliope, we thank you for your divine inspiration to those that would speak the divine words of the gods for the rest of us to hear. For without your blessing, we would be lost without the gods guidance of where our path is taking us.

Day Thirty One
Calypso
Nymph who lives in Ogygia

Calypso, she of sweet song. She who conceals. We are blessed when you are near and we are able to hear your glorious melodies that spill forth from your lips. We ask that after your time with us, you allow us to go on our way with the tools we need, for you are truly generous. You self sacrifice of your own happiness for the benefit of others shall always be remembered and used as a lesson to ourselves on how to improve our own sacrifices as well.

Day Thirty Two
Castor
Deity who helps shipwrecked sailors/ grants favorable winds/ Twin to Pollux

Castor, help those who have lost their way. When the day seems darkest and there is no escape to be found. May your favorable winds guide to safety. You hunted the boar, you sailed the Argo. We hope to find a minuscule of the courage you have. Keep us and guide us so the fates may grant us time to do so.

Day Thirty Three
Celano
One of the Pleiades

Celano, the dark one. Mother of kings. Companion of gods. As we gaze into the night sky to look upon you and your sisters, we would humbly ask that you bestow your favor upon us.

Day Thirty Four
Cerus
The bull tamed by Persephone

Cerus, the wild and untamable. Lets us be calmed like you were when we are feeling unrelenting rage. Let it fade away so we do not cause destruction. Let us learn patience and kindness as to be an example for others. We see your flowers in spring and your stars in fall.

Day Thirty Five
Ceto
Primordial sea goddess/ mother of sea monsters

Mighty Ceto, born from Gaia. We see you when the waves grow rough, when the churning waters threaten. MAy your children not choose to take us to an early grave unless your waters are being harmed.

Day Thirty Six

Cerberus

The three headed hound that guards the entrance to the underworld

Mighty Cerberus, he of three heads, companion to Hades and guardian of the underworld. We enter your gates with the upmost respect. Please allow us to pass unscathed so we may be judged and enter our afterlife.

Day Thirty Seven
Chaos
Primordial god that everything originated from

Mighty and everlasting Chaos, the eternal nothingness that our mortal minds cannot truly comprehend. Everything is and was born from you as it shall always be. We praise you. You reign over all. The cosmos owe themselves to you as do each and every one of us.

Day Thirty Eight
The Charities
Goddesses of charm/ beauty/ nature/ creativity/ fertility

Charities, bring beauty to our lives. Fill our days with good cheer and our nights with splendor. May we always be able to see how wonderful life can be, with your blessings.

Day Thirty Nine
Charon
The ferryman of the underworld

Charon, who meets us at the shores of the river once we have passed from this life. We humbly ask that you accept our loved ones, and us as well once our time has come. We pay you in coin as to have safe passage and we beg of you to provide it.

Day Forty

Chronos

God of time, turns the zodiac wheel

Chronos, god of time. We ask of you to slow the moments we cherish and to quicken our moments of pain and anguish. We as mortals depend on time and therefore depend on you.

Day Forty One
Chrysaor
Son of Poseidon and Medusa/ brother to Pegasus

Chrysaor, he born from Gorgon and god. He who carries the golden sword. Though your stories may not be known widely, we remember you. He who was born from blood.

Day Forty Two
Circe
Minor goddess with vast knowledge of potions/herbs

Circe, she who carries great knowledge, guide us to find the things of this Earth that we require to do great magic. May those who offend you always take the form of what they truly are and may men who present themselves with disgust always live their days in the mud and muck as the pigs they truly are.

Day Forty Three
Clio
The Muse of history

Clio, inspire us to never forget where we have come from so that we may see with clear eyes where we are headed. May the bloodshed of the past always be imprinted on us as a reminder to do better and create beauty.

Day Forty Four
Clotho
One of the fates/ the spinner

Clotho, we stand before you asking for your blessing. We ask that the thread you spin for us be strong and great in length. We wish to spend time on this plane, worshiping the gods and spreading the word of their greatness.

Day Forty Five
Creatures that serve the gods
All animals that serve the gods and perform tasks

Creatures of land, air, and sea. We honor you for performing the divine will of the gods. May they reward you for your undying loyalty.

Day Forty Six
Crios
The giant crab that guards the sea nymphs at Poseidon's palace

Crios, the immortal crab. Please protect us as you protect those in Poseidon's palace. If we are harmed, avenge us like you did when you killed Vamari.

Day Forty Seven
Cybele
Goddess of city walls/ fertile nature/ wild animals/ lions

Cybele, who travels from afar. She who brings with her mysteries and music. We ask of you to protect our lands. Make our lives fertile in every way and bestow upon us the strength of the lion.

Day Forty Eight
Cyclops
Forgers of the weapons of the gods

Mighty Cyclopi, those who work and toil to protect the gods. May you forever be remembered for your craftsmanship and skill. May the gods reward you in this life and the next.

Day Forty Nine

Demeter

Goddess of the harvest/ Earth/ fertility and grain

Demeter, keeper of the sacred law, goddess of the life cycle. Please take pity upon the mortals of this Earth. Allow our lands to be fertile and our grain to grow. There is no chance for life without your bountiful harvest.

Day Fifty
Dinlas
Guardian of Lamark where wounded heroes could heal after battle/ god of chaos/ hated

Dinlas, son of love and war. He who was abandoned and found. Keep from us your chaos and hatred. Be not led to destroy us. Instead, help our heroes find refuge to heal and we shall honor you.

Day Fifty One
Dionysus
God of the vine/ wine/ pleasure/ courage

Dionysus, god of the vine. Help us to find our courage in this life. Please make your gifts abundant to us so that we may taste the sweet fruits of mortality. May we celebrate you always for what you give to the world of men.

Day Fifty Two
Doris
Sea goddess/ mother to the nereids

Doris, mother to the spirits of the sea. May you and your children guide and protect us when we travel through perilous waters. Be they physical or spiritual.

Day Fifty Three
Echidna
An immortal monster of myth/ part female-part snake

Echidna, she who is immortal. Mother of many monsters. Without you, heroes have no purpose. Some of your children have and will always gain fame. You bring about the wildness of the world, showing what is truly possible.

Day Fifty Four
Eileithyia
Goddess of childbirth

Eileithyia, daughter of the king and queen of Olympus. Guide our children safely into this world. They are like one in a cave, coming towards the light. Please do not prevent or delay them from coming to us.

Day Fifty Five
Eirene
Goddess of peace

Eirene, bring peace to us and our families as you did for those in Athens. Each year that brings peace strengthens our reverence of your glory. For under your watchful hand, a bounty of prosperity is possible.

Day Fifty Six

Electra

One of the seven pleiades

Electra, She who carries a vengeful soul. Reach out to us when we have been hurt and when we have been wronged. Help us enact vengeance upon those who are deserving of it.

Day Fifty Seven
Elpis
The spirit of hope

Elpis, she who embodies hope. She, who was the last to leave Pandora's box. When toil and sickness rear their ugly heads, when disease and pain run rampant, allow us to see your comforting face. Let us feel your presence and know that not all is lost.

Day Fifty Eight
Elysium
Residence of the honored dead

Dwellers of Elysium, those who the gods chose to live peacefully in the afterlife. Just as you honored the gods, we honor you. May your eternal lives bring you true happiness and may you find your loved ones amongst the fields.

Day Fifty Nine
Enyo
Minor war goddess/ the spirit of war

Enyo, the mighty. Spirit goddess of war. Bring destruction to those who are deserving. May their high cities fall and your blood lust be quenched. But keep from our homes and our families so that war may not be incited by those who matter to us most.

Day Sixty

Eos

Goddess of dawn/ she who awakens us from sleep

Eos, mother of winds, dispenser of the morning dew. Each day is glorified as you ride your winged horses and we see your light. May your eternal lover Tithonus always be by your side in your journeys to come.

Day Sixty One

Epione

Goddess of soothing of pain

Epione, we call upon you when we are in pain. Please bring us relief. Please make our wounds heal and our pain fade. We thank you endlessly for your touch and blessing.

Day Sixty Two

Erato

The muse of lyrics/ love/ poetry

Erato, your beauty is heard in the singing of songs, in the words of love said to one another. You give life to our music and warm our hearts. May we think of you everytime a rhyme touches our ears.

Day Sixty Three
Erebus
God of darkness

Erebus, god of darkness. One of the first five to grace the world. You carry with you great power and great mystery. You take away the ugliness of the world and show us the beauty that resides in the skies. Let us not feel fear in your shadow, but embrace the darkness and all it holds for us.

Day Sixty Four
Eris
Goddess of strife/ discord

Eris, goddess of discord. We invite you to enter and walk wherever you please so you do not bring strife into our lives. May those who deny you experience true chaos.

Day Sixty Five
Eros
God of love/ sexual desire

Eros, born of the primordial. Let your arrows fly true. Do not leave us confused or wandering after unattainable love. May your Erotes follow your word for the continuation of mortals.

Day Sixty Six

Eurus

God of the east wind/ one of the Anemoi

Eurus, may your winds blow true. May we think of you when the leaves rustle and the birds fly through the air. We will not forget you as ancient writing did. We will honor you no matter the season.

Day Sixty Seven
Euterpe
Muse of music

Euterpe, giver of delight, you make each of our days brighter by providing the inspiration to millions to make beautiful music for the world to hear. Thank you for these sweet sounds for music truly gives breath to every way of life.

Day Sixty Eight
Gaia
Primordial goddess/ personification of Earth

Gaia, mother to us all. The one who keeps us and provides all we need. We thank you for your endless gifts. We stand in awe of your magnificence. We beg your forgiveness for those that abuse you and do not respect your power. Rise to greatness again mother, and show mortals your true power.

Day Sixty Nine

Glaucus

Sea god/ born mortal and turned immortal

Glaucus, eater of the magical herb. You understand a life of hard work and surviving on what you can. Bless us, and protect us from storms. Guide us to greatness as you were guided.

Day Seventy

Hades

God of the dead/ king of the underworld

Lord Hades, the rich god. He who travels in invisibility. All eventually come under your rule when the fates decide it. Please allow your hound to let us pass through your gates to be given a fair trial by your judges. May those who deserve it, be thrown into Tartarus, while those who lived for the gods be honored in Elysium. You are a mighty and powerful king who eventually oversees us all. May we forever praise you in the life that awaits.

Day Seventy One
Harmonia
Goddess of harmony/ concord

Harmonia, she who appears as a snake. Bring our lives into a state of harmony with the people and world around us. Let us not fall into a cursed way of living, but rather find concord with whoever will accept it.

Day Seventy Two
Harpocrates
The god of silence/ secrets

Harpocrates, child god of secrets. Help us when we need to be silent. Stop others from sharing our secrets that we tell them and help us to keep their secrets under lock and key. Teach us what is sacred and not to be shared.

Day Seventy Three

Hebe

Goddess of youth/ the prime of life/ forgiveness

Hebe, as we are not immortal, help us live in our prime for as long as we possibly can. Keep our bodies and minds youthful so that we may enjoy our mortal existence to the fullest. Give us the strength to forgive those that do not deserve it, to further ease the tiring hatred that can reside within our hearts.

Day Seventy Four
Hekate
Goddess of magic/ witchcraft/ crossroads

Hekate the triple goddess. We seek your never ending wisdom and guidance. May you come to us when we seek you at the crossroads. Teach us powerful magic so that we may create our own reality and find the power lurking within ourselves.

Day Seventy Five
Helios
God of the sun/ oaths/ sight

Helios, he who sees all. None can escape your gaze, be it god or man. May you illuminate our lives and help us see through the darkness. Press us to keep our oaths, as we are only as good as the promises we keep.

Day Seventy Six
Hemera
Primordial goddess of day

Hemera, Daughter of night. Guide us every day to make the most of our time and therefore our lives. We have much to do each day, but also help us to take time to enjoy every day and not feel as if all our time must be filled with work and toil.

Day Seventy Seven
Hephestus
God of fire/ blacksmithing

Hephestus, god of divine fire. May the gods always be armed to protect us and themselves. May your hearth always run hot and your hammer never miss. When we sharpen our blades, we do so in your name.

Day Seventy Eight
Hera
Queen of Olympus/ goddess of marriage/ women

Hera, our mighty queen. You rule on high over us all. May our unions always reflect your undying loyalty and may you bless us to be with who is meant for us. May you guide and protect the women that recognize you and keep them safe under your divine hands.

Day Seventy Nine
Heracles
Mortal hero turned god/ god of strength/ sports/ victory

Heracles, greatest of all heroes. He who shook the world with his strength and gained favor with his labors. Give us the strength to complete the tasks that face us within our own lives. Help us press forward and strive harder than we ever have before. Allow us to lay claim to our victories as you do so that we may be more like you.

Day Eighty

Hermes

God of travel/ commerce/ thieves/ trickery/ gambling/ guide to the underworld

Hermes, may you always walk beside us in our travels. Please keep us safe and by your side. May we trade and purchase knowing that we are not being stolen from. If we take a gamble, may it go in our favor and at our end, may we see you running towards us, so that we may be guided to the life that comes next.

Day Eighty One
Hesperus
The evening star

Hesperus, may you always shine bright and move quickly upon your journey in the sky. When we have occasion to see you, you are truly a magnificent sight to mortals everywhere.

Day Eighty Two
Hestia
Goddess of the home/ the hearth/ fertility/ family

Hestia, protector of our homes. We burn our hearths in your honor, whatever form they may take. Please protect our families and provide us with fertility in all aspects of life. We feel your presence when our families are brought together by your warmth.

Day Eighty Three
Huntresses of Artemis
Celebate virgins whose lives are dedicated to Artemis

To the Huntresses, those who hunt with the goddess of the moon. May you remain immortal and by her side forever in your divine mission.

Day Eighty Four
Hundred Handed Ones
Primordial children with fifty heads and one hundred hands

Mighty hundred handed ones. You were freed and fought alongside the gods in the great Titanomachy. Now you perform the sacred duty of guarding the overthrown titan lord in Tartarus so that we may never have to witness another titan - god war. Watch him sharply and true so he may never escape his bonds.

Day Eighty Five
Hygea
Goddess of cleanliness/ hygiene

Hygea, help us to achieve cleanliness, not only of our mortal bodies, but also of our immortal souls. For when we are clean, we are also at peace. A clean soul, free of hatred and jealousy will be our guide to bliss in the life that comes after this one.

Day Eighty Six
Hymenaios
God of marriage ceremonies

Hymenaios, make our unions joyful, filled with song and feasting. Allow our wedding night to be the same , filled with the songs of ecstasy, and feasting upon each other. May your wings cover and protect us from jealousy or ill will in the years to come.

Day Eighty Seven
Hypnos
Primordial god of sleep

Hypnos, he who lives in complete darkness. Bring us the deep sleep we need and desire, but allow us to wake from this living form of death. Furthermore, help us to find the secrets that linger in the darkness.

Day Eighty Eight
Iris
Goddess of the rainbows/ messenger of the gods

Iris, when we see your bright colors, please bring to us the messages from the gods that we need to hear. Thank you for your guidance and work, for if we are cut off from divinity, we are truly lost.

Day Eighty Nine
Judges of the underworld
Those who judge the afterlife you deserve

Judges, Rhadamanthys, Minos, and Aeacus. Judge us fairly. Let our good deads speak over our evil actions. We have strived for a life that would lead to Elysium. We have strived to honor and serve the gods. May we pass into a life such as this for all eternity.

Day Ninety
Khione
Goddess of snow

Khione, she who brings snow to cover our lands. We marvel in your beauty. Whenever you appear, you take away the ugliness of the mortal world and show us what Earth untouched by human hands can look like. Your power is great and because of that we ask that you keep your full strength at bay so that we may not perish from your great force.

Day Ninety One
Kindly Ones
The furies/ goddesses of vengeance against oath breakers/ protectors of children

Kindly Ones, we pray that we always keep our oaths so that we shall never have to come face to face with you. Punish those who incite your wrath. Exact your fierce punishment against any who do not keep their word and any who would harm a child.

Day Ninety Two
Kotys
Goddess of fertility/ sex

Kotys, your festivals have ended. Your rituals have ceased, but we worship you here and now. Let us bathe and cleanse ourselves in your name before participating in sexual acts for your glory. The night carries your name and we revel in it.

Day Ninety Three
Kratos
God of strength/ power

Kratos, he who stood with Zeus to defend Mount Olympus. He who would not flee from Typhon. Bring us great strength and lend us a grain of your power to complete all of our endeavors. Help us to overcome those who would stand against us.

Day Ninety Four
Kronos
Leader of the titans

Kronos, the god eater who separated heaven from Earth. You stood great when you stood against the primordials, but your power grew out of control. Overthrown by the gods and left in Tartarus. May you find peace within yourself and with your son.

Day Ninety Five

Lachesis

The Fate that measures the life thread

Lachesis, we seek you out to humbly ask to measure our thread long if it is your will to do so. We wish to live long lives before our thread is cut and so we request this from you. We however recognize that neither man nor god defies the fates and what they have in store must be honored.

Day Ninety Six
Maia
One of the pleiades/ goddess of fields

Maia, who blesses our fields and our children. Help us to succeed where we would otherwise fail. Be it in the growing of our crops or of our own children. Nurture our young with us so they may have great lives.

Day Ninety Seven
Mania
Goddess of the crazed/ mentally ill

Mania, your touch reaches many in this world, showing them a reality that others cannot fathom or understand. Please give strength to those struggling every day to merely survive in this world and help those that struggle, leading them to the help that they require.

Day Ninety Eight
Medusa
Gorgon who could turn those that looked upon her to stone

Medusa, protect us from those who would do us harm. Make them stop in their paths and be frozen in fear. Thank you for your protection and strength. You were mortal in life, but immortal to all those who know your name. You, mighty gorgon, shall live forever.

Day Ninety Nine
Melpomene
The muse of tragedy

Melpomene, you show us the balance of this world and bring us to our senses that we cannot spend our whole lives living in bliss. Things will crumble and be destroyed. May we learn from you how to pick up the pieces when tragedy strikes our own lives.

Day One Hundred

Merope

One of the pleiads/ goddess of natural forces/ rivers/ trees/ lakes/ mountains

Merope, whose spirit is seen in the mighty mountains, the strong trees, and the unstoppable rivers. We shall recognize you whenever we are in natural surroundings. We shall hear your voice clearly through all that we see and hear.

Day One Hundred and One
Metis
Titan goddess of wisdom

Metis, who dwells inside Zeus. Our lady of divine wisdom. You were treated unfairly by being swallowed up, but in this way, you are able to bring wisdom to all of Olympus. How can we ever thank you enough for making the gods wise and handing down their wisdom to us? Let us worship you through study and knowledge so that we may try to achieve even a small part of the wisdom you hold.

Day One Hundred and Two
Momus
God of satire/ writers/ poets

Momus, you give us entertainment. You provide us with books of history and fantasy. Most importantly, the words of poets from antiquity. Without these, we would have no basis for our worship. Thank you for your divine inspiration given to those that we needed to write their words, instead of just speaking them. Thank you for showing us that through this hard life, we can still find humor and laugh at ourselves.

Day One Hundred and Three
Morpheus
God of dreams

Morpheus, you guide us into the dream world to live lives of fantasy and receive messages to influence our waking lives. If it is your will, allow us to be lucid so that we may partake in the dreamscape and make our time with you even more meaningful.

Day One Hundred and Four
Nemesis
Goddess of vengeance/ retribution

Nemesis, if they are deserving, let those who stand against us come into your path. May your vengeance be swift and strong against them and all others in this world whose only aim is to hurt and to take advantage of others.

Day One Hundred and Five
Nereus
Titan god of the sea/ wisdom/ prophecy/ shapeshifting

Nereus, old man of the sea. Let us see your messages in the thrashing waves. May you appear before us in whatever shape you wish to bring us these messages of what is to come, for you are truly wise and we desire to hear you speak.

Day One Hundred and Six
Nike
Goddess of victory

Nike, we see your name in much abundance throughout our entire world. We implore you to bring us individual victory and victory to the gods against all that would dare stand against us and them. May we hear the flap of your wings in our times of need and may you always lead us down the right path.

Day One Hundred and Seven
Notus
The south wind/ bringer of storms

Notus, the mighty south wind, bringer of storms in summer and autumn. You choose to make us warm or cold, to keep our lands dry or to pound them with rain. When the south wind howls, we hear your voice. When the leaves are plucked from the trees and blown to the ground underneath a gray sky, we know you are near.

Day One Hundred and Eight
Nymphs of non fame
Nymphs that were not given their own stories

Nymphs of the world, though you may not have a story that stood the test of time, we honor you. We honor your service, your power, and your domains, be they on land or at sea. Feel our prayers, for you are remembered.

Day One Hundred and Nine

Nyx

Goddess of night

Nyx, neverending night. We witness you at the end and beginning of every day. As the sun is lowered and before it rises our whole reality is in your domain. You rule over all, casting yourself into every corner and crevice. All nocturnal creatures are under your will and praise you by living in your world.

Day One Hundred and Ten
Oceanus
Titan god of the ocean

Oceanus, your power is present when the sea spirals out of control. When storms rage and waters swirl. When we as mortals observe the waters and know that they are truly uncontrollable, we know this is due to your power.

Day One Hundred and Eleven
Pallas
Titan god of war

Pallas, we desire you to rest. To offer us peace from the bloodshed and pain that we inflict upon each other. May you sleep long and deep so that we may learn how to release our hate and finally dwell peacefully amongst each other.

Day One Hundred and Twelve
Pan
God of woods/ fields/ flocks/ the wild

Pan, he who is over all that is wild. He that has unbridled lust. Let us feel your panic at times of pleasure instead of in times of fear. Join us in our sexual exploits so that you may also feel pleasure. Please guard the wild places of this world always so they may stay untouched by man.

Day One Hundred and Thirteen
Pegasus
Divine winged horse

Pegasus, he who takes to the air, born from the neck of your mother. Mighty son of Poseidon. Please carry our messages to the gods so that they may hear our words. Help us to defeat the monsters in life that seek us out.

Day One Hundred and Fourteen
Peitho
Goddess of persuasion/ seduction

Peitho, she who holds the keys to seduction and love. Protect us from being persuaded under false pretenses or for malicious means. Allow us to only persuade and seduce when our intentions are pure and they will not affect another negatively, but enhance their lives for the better.

Day One Hundred and Fifteen
Persephone
Goddess of spring/ queen of the underworld

Persephone, she who brings life to death. Mighty queen of the underworld. May you watch over us once we pass from this life as our queen and protector. While we are still here, may we learn the divine lesson of rebirth from you every year when you turn a landscape of death into one that lives again.

Day One Hundred and Sixteen

Pheme

Goddess of fame/ nobility/ scandalous rumors

Pheme, she who spreads words about all. Please keep us in your favor and make us known for the good that we have done. Let us not fall from your grace and have words spread that will only hurt and hinder us, but to have our names live forever and be thought of in good memory.

Day One Hundred and Seventeen
Phosphorus
The morning star

Phosphorus, the bright morning star. You teach us of the cycle of rebirth after spiritual death. May we keep our eyes and ears open to better learn this lesson of endings and beginnings.

Day One Hundred and Eighteen
Plutus
God of abundance/ wealth/ riches

Plutus, he who carries the cornucopia of abundance. Help us to find wealth in this world. Not just in monetary form, but in family and experience. For we know that not all riches can be counted and stored. We know real wealth is found in the lives we lead.

Day One Hundred and Nineteen
Pollux
One of the twins of Gemini

Pollux, he of great strength. Teach us how to be dedicated to the ones we love. Just as you appealed to Zeus to make your brother immortal. Let us always appeal to the gods on behalf of the ones we love.

Day One Hundred and Twenty
Polyhymnia
One of the muses over sacred poetry/ geometry

Polyhymnia, keeper of sacred secrets. We use your blessings to encode this world with great knowledge and information for those who are worthy to find it. You help us understand our planet and its sacred sites so that we as mortals, may better worship the gods.

Day One Hundred and Twenty One
Pontus
Primordial sea god of the deep sea

Pontus, he born of only mother. He who came out of the primordial to show us not all roads are made from dirt and stone, but also the great sea may serve as our road for travel and trade. Protect us as we travel in your realm and lead us to safe harbors.

Day One Hundred and Twenty Two
Poseidon
God of the sea/ earthquakes/ horses

Mighty Poseidon, king of Earth, god of the sea, mighty Earth shaker. Master of the seas and all its creatures. We stand in awe of your might. Protect us and keep us. Let our enemies feel your rage and cower before your name. When horses run, we know your power and when the sea rages, we know your might.

Day One Hundred and Twenty Three
Priapus
God of gardens/ fertility

Priapus, we stand in awe of your presence. Make our gardens flourish and our lives fertile. We thank you for your blessings and when things grow, may we praise your name.

Day One Hundred and Twenty Four
Pricus
Father of sea goats

Pricus, father of the amazing sea goats favored by the gods. He who has power over time itself. We pray that not all your children reach the shores and lose their fish tails. We pray that they always maintain their ability to think and speak, so they may continue to honor you.

Day One Hundred and Twenty Five
Prometheus
Titan who stole fire from Olympus/ created humans
clay

Prometheus, the tortured. He who created us and gave us fire. We owe our lives and civilizations to you. Your sacrifice caused you much pain, but we pray that Zeus may forgive your transgressions. For without us, there is no worship of the gods.

Day One Hundred and Twenty Six
Proteus
A manifestation of Nereus/ titan god of the sea/ wisdom/ prophecy/ shapeshifting

Proteus, old man of the sea. Let us see you in all your forms. May you appear before us in whatever shape you wish to bring us your messages of what is to come. The fish of the deep, or the animals that crawl out of the water to live upon land. In all of these we shall look for your presence and keep our ears open for what you have to tell us.

Day One Hundred and Twenty Seven
Rhea
Mother of the gods

Rhea, she who saved all the gods from their titan father. Protect us as you would protect your own children. Lead us all to glory by fostering the relationships between gods and mortals. Make us of one family, always helping and loving each other.

Day One Hundred and Twenty Eight
Selene
Goddess of moonlight/ mother of vampires

Selene, she who carries the light of the moon to us. She whose blood was blessed and drunk by Endymion to create an immortal race. The night is truly the realm of you and your children. May they carry the legacy of your blood and name forever.

Day One Hundred and Twenty NIne
Sterope
One of the pleiades/ mother of Ares

Sterope, she who burns bright in the sky. She who bore the essence of war into this world. Please hold us in your favor. May you always look down kindly upon us and not allow war to come to our doorstep.

Day One Hundred and Thirty
Styx
Goddess of the river styx/ oaths/ first to stand with the gods against the titans

Styx, she who aided Zeus in the great war. Let our loyalty to the gods always be like your own. Let us never break a sacred vow made on your river, or so shall we face the wrath of the gods.

Day One Hundred and Thirty One
Tartarus
God of the depths of the underworld

Tartarus, your name strikes fear into all that hear it. May we live lives that do not lead us into your eternal storm. We thank you for holding the beats and monsters of this world, whether they be mortal or divine.

Day One Hundred and Thirty Two
Taygete
One of the seven pleiades/ mistress of animals

Taygete, she who bears golden horns. You run amongst the animals of the mountain and allow us to see you in every animal we encounter. With them, may we send praise to you, the mother of Sparta.

Day One Hundred and Thirty Three
Terpsichore
The muse of dancing

Terpsichore, let us revel in your sweet song and express the emotions it fills us with in dance. You give our mortal bodies beauty and skill so that we may show it to each other and express ourselves for you and the gods.

Day One Hundred and Thirty Four
Thalia
The muse of comedy

Thalia, you inspire one of the best things in mortal life. You make us laugh and feel joy. We thank you endlessly for this gift, for without it, there is no respite from our hard lives.

Day One Hundred and Thirty Five
Thanatos
God of death

Thanatos, he who meets us all. We may never see all the gods, but we know we shall see you when we enter eternal sleep. When our thread is cut, come to us swiftly so that we may enter the underworld and start life again.

Day One Hundred and Thirty Six
Themis
Titan goddess of divine order/ law/ justice

Themis, she who carries the sword and the scales. She who is not swayed. Bring justice into our lives when we are deserving of it. When chaos reigns, may your steady hand bring us back to a place of order.

Day One Hundred and Thirty Seven
Thetis
Goddess of the sea/ leader of the nereides

Thetis, she who sees what is to come. Shapeshifter and bearer of sons who surpass their fathers. We honor you whenever we see a creature dip below the waves and another come up in its place. This is a sign we recognize as you are with us.

Day One Hundred and Thirty Eight
Triton
Messenger of the sea

Triton, son of the king and queen of the deep. Blow your conch shell so that all may hear. Carry the words of mighty Poseidon to us all and if our words are deemed worthy, carry them back to him to hear our prayers and praises.

Day One Hundred and Thirty Nine
Tyche
Goddess of good and bad fortune/ prosperity

Tyche, she who chooses if we prosper or fail. Bring us good fortune if we are deserving. We shall realize when there is a turn of circumstance for the better, that you have blessed us and when it is for the worst, to appease you and find how we have fallen from your favor.

Day One Hundred and Forty
Typhon
Titan god of monsters/ storms/ volcanoes

Typhon, he who strikes fear into all. Realize your place within the pantheon and do not bring challenge to the gods. Instead, work with them so that this world may experience peace.

Day One Hundred and Forty One
Urania
The muse of astrology

Urania, she who inspires us to look to the stars. You help us to understand ourselves and what is to come. May we only hear those that speak your true words and not false seers who exploit for profit in your name. May we always look to the skies and feel your presence.

Day One Hundred and Forty Two
Uranus
Primordial god of the sky/ father to all titans

Uranus, the great sky. The one that is above us all. May your spirit be calm after the violence that befell you. May you not rage and send the world into storms. May you and Gaea find peace with each other now that the reign of titans has ceased.

Day One Hundred and Forty Three
Zelus
The god of zeal/ rivalry/ jealousy

Zelus, may our rivalries be positive ones, not meant to crush the spirit of another. May we not dwell in the darkness of jealousy, but do the work to improve our own lives. Fill our minds and hearts with zeal so that we may press forward in our pursuits.

Day One Hundred and Forty Four
Zephyrus
The west wind/ one of the anemoi

Zephyrus, the untamed. Your wind blows wild and drives us to feel the wild spirit of the world. May you find someone that loves you and not grow jealous of those that love another. Beat your mighty wings and bring in wonderful spring.

Day One Hundred and Forty Five
Zeus
King of Olympus/ leader of the gods/ god of lightning/ thunder/ the heavens

Mighty Zeus, he who rules over all. He who saved his brothers and sisters from the belly of his father. Mighty Lightning bearer who led the battle against the titans. We worship you on high as ruler of all Olympus. May nothing escape your watchful eye. May your bolts fly swift and strike true. You rule over us all and we sing praises to your name.

Day One Hundred and Forty Six
Those who are forgotten/ lost/ or unmentioned

To those who have been lost to time. To those who have not been mentioned. We offer you this prayer in an attempt to help you live on and survive. May you feel honored and full of joy.

Day One Hundred and Forty Seven
Those who watch over us

We offer up prayers to those who keep a close eye on our lives and our well being. Be it god of ancestor, we honor and thank you for the care you give us through our lives. Show us the paths to walk and help us be kind to all around us. May we honor you so completely that through your power and grace we become bright beacons in this dark world for others to follow.

May the gods always be with you and may you always walk amongst them.

Printed in Great Britain
by Amazon

44756940R00088